Everything Other Than Chess

by Claude Needham

Everything Other Than Chess

by Claude Needham

Gateways Books and Tapes

Nevada City, California

Typesetting by Claude Needham
Proofreading by Patricia Elizabeth, Rose Gander, Tabatha Jones
Cover design by iTRANSmedia

All rights reserved. Printed in the United States of America
Gateways Books and Tapes
P.O. Box 370
Nevada City, CA 95959
1-800-869-0658
http://www.gatewaysbooksandtapes.com
ISBN-10: 0-89556-145-X
ISBN-13: 978-0-89556-145-9

Library of Congress Cataloging-in-Publication Data

Needham, Claude, 1951-
  Everything other than chess / by Claude Needham.
      p. cm.
  ISBN 0-89556-145-X
  1. Board games. I. Title.
  GV1312.N44 2006
  794--dc22
                        2006014302
                         CIP

Table of Contents

Introduction

What do you do if you would like to own a chess set but don't want to learn chess?

Let's face it, chess sets are gorgeous. When it comes to style and grace, you can't beat a chess set for beauty and fine craftsmanship. Rarely will a game approach the artistic heights that a chess set can inspire. World famous artists have sculpted individual pieces and mints have issued limited edition castings. From simple to fair and fair to exquisite, chess sets are sights to behold.

There's only one itsy bitsy little problem with owning a chess set—chess sets are made for playing chess. "Not a problem for chess players," you say. But what if you don't aspire to being a chess player? One solution—often used—is just to leave the game around the house on a pedestal or coffee table and enjoy it as sculpture. That is one solution.

There is an even better answer. And, this book is that answer. Within its pages you'll find games designed to be played on a chessboard with chess pieces, only these games are *everything other than chess*.

We've included games of strategy and games of pure dumb luck. There are games for adults and games suitable for children of all ages. Some of the games are simple chase games and others are elaborate capture challenges. A bit of this and a bit of that. Basically *everything other than chess*—as promised.

A few of the games require a modicum of additional equipment. Below is a list of all the additional equipment you might need for any of the games in this book:

Six-sided die. You'll need two (2) dice.

Eight-sided die. You'll need two (2) of these.

Counting stones, or buttons, beans or other small lumps.

Pencil and pad.

Small stickers or dots.

A twenty-sided (d20) die. You'll need one (1) or these.

Add to this a sense of fun, creativity, wonder, delight and oh yes... maybe a few refreshments, and you're bound to have a great time.

Enjoy.

Ants and the Cake

Everyone loves a picnic—especially ants. And the picnic yummy that ants love the very best is cake. Let's face it... ants love cake.

But cake is too big for one ant to carry alone. That is why ants cooperate. Ants are very good at cooperating—at least with members of their own anthill. But they don't do so well at cooperating with ants from other anthills. This is why when a piece of cake is left after a big picnic, ant clans fight so hard to get the cake for themselves.

That is the basis of "Ants and the Cake"—two groups of ants fighting for a single piece of cake.

Object of the game: Capture the cake for your anthill and your family of ants.

Additional equipment: One six-sided die.

Board setup: The back row for each player (row 1) represents the anthill. Each player puts 8 ants in this "anthill" row.

After it is decided which player goes first, the other player will place a queen in the very center of the board to represent the cake. Or, if you prefer, a candy, small piece of cake or other treat may be placed in the center of the board instead of the queen. In either case this will be the prized "Cake" which the ants shall fight over. Keep in mind that placing the "cake" in the center of the board means it will not be in a square; it will be on the lines between squares.

How to play: To start the game, players decide who goes first. This can be by mutual agreement, or loser goes first, or youngest first, or highest roll on a six-sided die goes first, or arm wrestling for all I care. Just figure out who is going first, otherwise, you'll end up sitting there like lumps all day waiting to get started.

At the beginning of each turn, a player rolls a six-sided die. The number on the die will tell the player how many ants to move that turn. Each ant moves one (1), and only one (1) square each turn. This means that on any given turn (depending on the luck of the roll) a player may move six (6) ants or a player may move only one (1) ant. It all depends on luck.

Ants may move forward, backward, left or right. Ants may not move diagonally. No diagonal moves are allowed.

During the game, ants from each player will try to sneak up on the cake and grab it before the other ants do.

A player may not put two of her ants on the same square.

However, if a player's ant moves into a square occupied by an opposing ant, then the opposing ant is sent back to its starting line (anthill). The ant that is sent back is put into any empty square closest to the center of the anthill.

When an ant is taken, the victorious ant is said to be "hot." A "hot" ant may be counterattacked immediately by any adjacent ants from the other anthill—if the defending player so chooses. This will happen right in the middle of the attacking player's turn even before the rest of her moves are completed. This creates a rapid exchange of attacks and counterattacks.

The defending player must decide without delay and the counterattack happens at that very moment—even before the attacking player finishes her moves. If the defending player does choose to counterattack her ant then becomes "hot." This exchange of attack and counterattack happens right in the middle of a turn. When all adjacent ants are gone or a player declines to counterattack, the original player completes her turn.

Let's look at an example of how attacks and counterattacks work with "hot" ants. Assume that the Black ant (a) moves onto the square occupied by the White ant (b) sending it back to the anthill. The Black ant (a) is now "hot." White may choose to counterattack this "hot" ant or may choose not to counterattack. In our example, White decides to counterattack Black ant (a) using the White ant (c).

Thus, White ant (c) takes Black ant (a) leading to the configuration of ants as seen on the right. After taking ant (a) the White ant (c) is now "hot." And so the battle continues, since given the choice, Black decides to attack her opponent's "hot" ant with the Black ant (d).

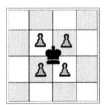

Black ant (d) takes White ant (c) leading to the new arrangement as seen on the left. At this point, Black ant (d) is "hot." And so the carnage continues as White ant (e) jumps at the chance to take Black ant (d). This once again leaves the White ant (e) as "hot." But, alas, there are no adjacent ants to attack, counterattack, or counter-counterattack.

As you can see in the image to the right, with no remaining ants to attack, the "hot" spell ends allowing Black to finish whatever is left of the turn.

How to win: To capture the cake all that is required is for a player to surround the cake (queen) with four ants. When the cake is surrounded by four ants of the same color the cake is captured, carried away, and eaten by those ants... yum.

Multiple players: For instructions on how to play this game with more than two players, watch for a future expanded edition of this book.

Jousting

There's nothing quite like the thrill of watching full grown men climb upon massive horses and gallop full speed toward each other waving great, huge sticks ready to knock the other from his steed into the mud and horse poop.

Noble men and noble women of the Middle Ages were much amused by these "Jousting" matches. And for those not lucky enough to be born during the time of rampant state sanctioned ignorance and plague, there is always the historical re-enactment societies of today.

This game, coincidentally also called "Jousting," is the chessboard non-chess game equivalent of the Middle Ages sport. Our game is guaranteed to be packed with the same thrills and chills, excitement and spills, everything except for the mud and horse poop. That you'll have to either do without or supply on your own.

Or, if you prefer genuine *Everything other than Chess* brand mud and horse poop, contact us and we'll be glad to package some up and send it your way—for a minor fee, of course.

Object of the game: Win more jousting matches than your opponent.

Additional equipment: Two six-sided dice and a bag of counting stones.

Board setup: The back row for each player (row 1) represents

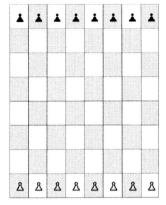

the starting gate for the knights in the jousting tournament. Each player places eight (8) knights (pawns) in this row.

How to play: Players decide who goes first.

A player begins a turn by rolling two (2) six-sided die. That player then selects two of her jousters and moves them according to the roll of the dice.

A player may move either two jousters (one for each die) or a single jouster (using the sum of the dice).

A jouster may not move past an opponent's piece.

Jouster's move in a forward direction only.

If there is no jouster that may move the specified number of squares that die is forfeit for that turn and only one jouster moves. Or, if it is not possible to use either of the die rolls, then the player gets to move none of his jousters that turn.

If a jouster lands on an opponent's piece that jousting match goes to (i.e. is won by) the player whose jouster lands upon the opponent's jouster.

When a joust is won the winning player takes a token (bean or other marker) from the common pile to denote the win.

Each player will maintain a clearly visible pile of counters. This helps nervous types keep track of how far ahead or how far behind they are.

After a joust is won the two pieces from that joust are returned to their respective home row squares. All other pieces are left on the board as they are. Only the two pieces from the joust in question are returned.

A roll of six (6) is special. A player rolling six may choose to use it as normal—moving a jouster six squares. Or, a player may choose to use a roll of six (6) to reset a joust. Resetting a joust means that the two pieces on that column are returned to their beginning squares. Once the jousting pieces are returned to their respective home squares, that joust is treated as any other joust.

A player rolling a six may reset a joust with the six then use the remaining die to move the jouster from the freshly reset column.

How to win: The first player to win 20 jousts is declared the winner with all appropriate bragging rights.

Multiple players: It is possible to play Joust with 2, 4, 6 or 8 players. When playing with two, each player has eight (8) jousters on her side. When playing with four, each player has four (4) jousters under her control. When playing with six, or eight, we recommend dividing into two teams of either three for four respectively. These teams can then argue endlessly about what to do before making a move. This should provide endless fun for those watching the game and might even lead to a few jousting matches right there in the living room.

Example Move: If it happens to be White's turn, a roll of three would win the joust in the second column, a roll of two would win the joust in the third column, a roll of five would win the joust in the fourth column, and a roll of four would win the joust in the eight column. Or, one could combine both dice to achieve a role of seven to win jousts in column one, five, or seven.

Scatter

Remember entering the kitchen late at night? As you walk into the dark room, find the wall switch and turn on the light, a squadron of multi-legged creatures scatter for safety in the dark recesses of the room.

That's exactly what the game of *Scatter* is like. Players start by placing eight bugs each in the middle of the "floor." After all the bugs are placed in the open, the game begins—a mad dash toward the safety of the dark squares on the edge of the board.

Object of the game: Get your eight "bugs" (pawns) to the safety of the dark squares on the edge of the "floor" (board).

Additional equipment: No additional equipment required.

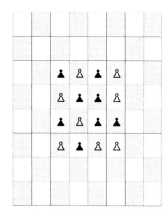

Board setup: Play begins with a blank board—no bugs present. During the setup phase of the game, players take turns adding "bugs" piece by piece until the center (four by four square) is filled.

The board to the left is an example of what a setup may look like after "bugs" are placed on the board. Each game setup will be different depending upon how participating players choose to place their "bugs".

How to play: Players decide who goes first. This can be either by agreement or the rolling of a six-sided die to see who rolls highest or whatever.

The first thing players do is add "bugs" to the center of the board until each player has eight "bugs" on the board—as described under board setup.

When this setup phase is finished, the center of the "floor" will be filled with bugs—eight white and eight black.

After the setup is complete, imagine someone has walked into the kitchen and turned on the light—now the scatter begins.

Think of the scatter phase of the game as the reaction of the bugs on the kitchen floor to the light being turned on. The bugs run for the safety of the edge—in this case, any one of the fourteen (14) dark squares (indicated by √) on the side of the chessboard.

During the scatter phase, each player moves one bug per turn. A bug may be moved one square (up, down, left, right, or diagonally).

In addition to simple one square moves, a bug may jump other bugs. In fact, a bug may perform several consecutive jumps if the opportunity presents it self.

A jump is allowed provided there is an empty space on the opposite side of an adjacent piece (either your own or your opponent's). In the sample game to the right, let's look at a jump possible for the Black piece, in Black's row five (5) column six (6). (Recall that from White's perspective this would be row four (4) column three (3). The piece in question could jump, in one single turn, first to 1, then to 2, then 3, then finally to four. This

Part way through a game.

may or may not be a wise move. The point here is that it is a legal move.

How to win: To win the game, be the first to get your eight bugs into dark squares on the edge of the board. Actually, it is not a question of being first. Since there are sixteen bugs and only fourteen dark edge squares, if you get your eight bugs to safety, your opponent will be left with two bugs standing around in the middle of the floor. Thus, your bugs will have reached the relative safety of dark corners away from the light. And, your opponent's bugs face the dangers of the dreaded kitchen floor in the light.

If both players manage to get seven bugs each into the edge squares the game is declared a draw.

Multiple players: Scatter may be played by two or four players. The two player version is as described above. In the four player version of the game, one may either play as teams in which each team member takes alternate turns moving the "bugs". Or, by adding pieces from a second (differently colored) chess set, each of four players may control four of the sixteen bugs.

When playing with four—not in team mode—there will be more than one player getting all four of her bugs home.

In this case, the first player to get her bugs to safety is the first place winner, the second player to get her bugs to safety is the second place winner, and so on.

Night Bombing

It is a well known fact, at least in science fiction circles, that certain advanced races have mastered the art of guiding meteorites from space to land with a fiery vengeance upon their enemies—a rain of terror from above—like weapons. These advanced races (typically alien) influence the fall of incoming meteorites through mystical mental powers left unexplained—especially since special effects in the 1950s were not up to the standards of today. Apart from the cost savings of using floating debris from space as weapons, this method of warfare has two minor drawbacks: 1) it must be done at night, 2) it's not very accurate as a weapon and you run a very real risk of hitting your own people. Well, dem's da breaks. At least you are not bombing your own people with bombs costing millions to build. And it might be a good thing to clean up space removing all of the floating rocks and such.

Object of the game: Bomb five of your opponent's pieces before five of your own pieces are blown to bits.

Additional equipment: Two eight-sided dice.

Board setup: Play begins with an empty board. During the first phase of game play, players take turns placing pieces one at a time on the board (one per turn) until all thirty-two (32) pieces, are positioned on the game board. Each player uses all sixteen (16) of her pieces making for a total of thirty-two (32) targets.

After all of these targets are placed upon the board, the second phase of game play begins: players start raining meteorites down upon each other's heads.

How to play: To drop a meteorite a player rolls two eight-sided dice. These two dice will be the row and column coordinates of the bomb.

The row/column numbers for each player is relative to that player's point of view. The column count begins with one (1) on the left and ends with eight (8) on the right. The row count begins with row one (1) nearest the player and ends with row eight (8) on the far side of the board. Thus, row one for a player will be an opponent's row eight—and vice versa.

A player has the choice of which eight-sided dice is the row and which eight-sided die is the column. This gives a player marginal control over the meteorite's coordinates—hopefully making it possible to avoid one's own pieces.

If the meteorite drops on an opponent's piece, the piece is placed in a victory pile.

If a meteorite drops upon a player's own piece it goes into the "oops" pile.

Every piece in a player's oops pile counts as half a piece against pieces in her victory pile. Thus, if a player has two pieces in her oops pile then she will need to collect six pieces (five plus one extra to compensate for the 2 oops) in the victory pile in order to win.

Only pieces in your victory pile count toward the calculation of winning scores.

How to win: Players win by collecting pieces in their victory piles. The first to reach a victory count of five (5) wins. Keep in mind that each "oops" piece counts as ½ against the victory count. In a time limited game the player with the higher count wins.

Black's Side

White's Side

Example Play: The image on the left illustrates the starting position for the example.

Assume the following moves:

White (1,3) ♟
Black (4,2) ♞
White (8,2) miss
Black (7,2) ♕
White (6,4) ♚
Black (8,2) miss.

At this point the game would be tied. Each player has managed to guide meteorites into two of the opponent's pieces—along with one miss each. The new board position is detailed in the image on the next page.

Let's assume, White's next roll was a two, two (2,2). In this case, White cannot escape sending a meteorite slamming into one of her own pieces. Bad luck. Guess that's what you get for using unwieldy, clumsy meteorites for weapons.

Multiple players: This game will work with two, three, four, or more players. Pieces from additional chess sets may be added.

If the board becomes too crowded, then players may elect to use only eight targets each.

When playing as teams, team members should combine bombed pieces into a common victory pile—one for each team.

Kingdoms

Wouldn't life be grand if neighboring kingdoms weren't always trying to overthrow your government and kill the king? Perhaps, but then where would we find the inspiration behind so many nifty games, television shows, and potential movie plots.

Object of the game: Kill your opponent's King, or at least enough pieces to make it impossible for your opponent to kill your King.

Additional equipment: No additional equipment required.

Board setup: The game begins with an empty board.

During the first phase of game, players take turns placing pieces on the board (one per turn) until all thirty-two (32) pieces (sixteen per side) are positioned on the game board. Each player may place her pieces on any empty square within the first three rows.

How to play: Players decide who goes first. Use whichever method you prefer to decide.

Each turn a player will make two moves: 1) move a soldier one square, 2) move the king one square.

This pacing back and forth by the king could be attributed to

Claude Needham

natural worry about the advancing enemy, or it could be simply nervous energy. In either case, if the king is put into a position such that it cannot pace, the player will forfeit the game.

The king's move is one square (forward, backward, left, or right—not diagonal).

The soldier's move is one square (forward, backward, left, or right—not diagonal).

If a piece moves onto a square occupied by an enemy soldier, hand-to-hand combat between the two pieces ensues. The outcome of this fight is decided by the rank of the pieces involved—tie going to the advancing active piece.

King   – may win against (none)

Queen   – may win against (Q, B, Kn, P)

Bishop   – may win against (B, Kn, P)

Knight   – may win against (Kn, P)

Pawn   – may win against (P, Q)

Rook   - immovable, cannot be attacked.

Note 1: You'll notice that the king is pretty much worthless in actual combat. He's mostly trained to give orders to his own soldiers.

Note 2: When the queen jumps a pawn, the pawn is defeated as in normal combat leaving the queen to occupy the newly emptied square. However, if a pawn advances on a queen, both the queen and pawn disappear. It's not known if they both die in combat or run off to some romantic hideaway. All those left behind on the battlefield know for sure is: the square previously occupied by the queen is now empty.

As noted above, the rook is a special piece which acts like a bit of castle. It is immovable and may not be moved once the setup phase of the game is over. Also none of the other pieces may attack the castle (rook).

How to win: There are two methods of winning. One can either capture the opponent's king, or, one can create a situation in which the opponent's king is prevented from pacing. Since the king cannot beat any of the soldiers in hand-to-hand combat, the king may not advance onto a square occupied by an enemy piece. The king is also prevented from advancing on any of his own soldiers. So getting hemmed-in is a very real danger for the king.

Multiple players: This is basically a two person game.

Claude Needham

Mountain Raid

A small band of rebels defending against a larger and better equipped advancing army is a common story repeating itself century after century—from Sparta to the Alamo. Sometimes they win; more often than not they lose. Such is the destiny of those who would stand against the tide.

In this game, four defending rebels stand at the top of the mountain working to keep an advancing force of seven brigands at bay. The brigands seem to pour forth in an endless stream.

The only hope the mountain rebels have is to send a man down the mountain to find help in the towns below. Perhaps he can reach the base of the mountain and get help before it is too late.

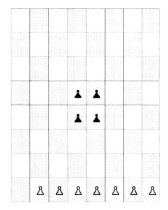

Additional equipment: One (1) six-sided die is used for movement.

Object of the game: The Black defenders work to get a man to the base of the mountain. The White brigands work to get a man into one of the four center squares.

Board setup: At the beginning of the game, four Black rebels stand ready at the center of the board to defend the mountaintop. Seven White brigands line up at the base of the mountain ready to race toward the center and victory at the top of the mountain.

How to Play: White and Black take turns.

At the beginning of a turn a player rolls one six-sided die. When it is White's turn the die indicates the number of squares to advance toward the top of the mountain (counter-clockwise); when it is Black's turn, the die indicates the number of squares to descend the mountain (clockwise).

Both White and Black must use the spiraling mountain path.

The image to the left illustrates the mountain path as used by White brigands on their climb up the mountain. White brigands start in the base row, at bottom, and move counter-clockwise up the mountain.

The image to the right illustrates the mountain path as used by Black rebels on their way to the base of the mountain. Black rebels start at the top of the mountain (the center of the board) and work their way down in a clockwise spiral.

The target destination of the Black rebel men is any of the seven squares in the first row marked as baserow. This represents the town where the rebels may find help.

The target destination of the White brigands is the top of the mountain (four center squares) marked with "◇".

Taking men: If White rolls a number that will have a brigand land on a rebel, then the rebel is removed from the game—reducing the number of rebels in the game. If Black rolls a number that will have a rebel land on top of a brigand, then the brigand is removed from the game—reducing the number or brigands in the game.

Brigands may land on brigands with no problem. And rebels may land on rebels with no problem.

How to win: If a White brigand reaches the top of the mountain (any of the "◇" squares in the center of the board) then White wins. If a Black rebel reaches town (any of the seven squares called the baserow) then Black win.

In case you haven't noticed, White has the definite advantage in this game. Players should either take turns being Black, or the better player should volunteer to play Black.

Multiple players: This game is made for two players.

Claude Needham

Horse Race

Horses, horses, and more horses. In this game they race around the track as fast as they can. First horse to travel one full circuit around the track gets to take the glorious walk into the winner's circle.

Object of the game: Get your horse around the track first.

Additional equipment: A six-sided die.

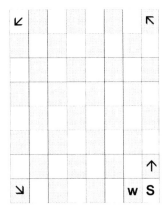

Board setup: The "**S**" marks the starting gate for both horses. Both horses stand side by side on this starting square.

How to play: Each turn a player will roll one (1) six-sided die. The horse is moved that number of squares around the outer edge.

Horses may share a square.

Horses go counter-clockwise.

How to win: The first horse to go around the board and get back to the "w" wins. Players are not required to roll an exact count to win. Any count that will move the horse past the "w" will win.

Multiple players: For Multiple players to play simply use different looking chess pieces to represent each horse. I suppose 16 or more could play. But, boy would they be crowded on the starting square.

Claude Needham

Two Furlongs

A furlong is a unit for measuring distance, equal to 1/8 mile (201 meters). The name comes from farming. A furrow is the long narrow trench (groove) made in the ground for planting on a farm. So a furlong is how long normal furrows were once upon a time. However, in modern times the place you are most likely to hear the word "furlong" is at the racing track, where we all know that furlongs are used to measure distance in horse races.

In our race track, once around the track is one furlong and twice around the track is two furlongs. Now, since the name of this game is "Two Furlongs," can you guess how many times the horses go around the track? If you guessed two, you win the beginning game quiz.

Object of the game: Get your horse around the outer and inner track first.

Additional equipment: Two six-sided dice for determining how far each horse moves during a turn.

Board setup: At the beginning of the race, the track (board) is empty.

All of the horses are off the board waiting right by the "**S**".

This "**S**" marks the starting square.

How to play: Players take turns rolling the dice to move their horses around the track. No special roll is required to start. Any roll of the dice will get a horse on the track and going.

⚑	2	2	2	2	2	⚐
2	⚑	1	1	1	1	⚐ 2
2	1				1	2
2	1				1	2
2	1				1	2
2	1				1	2
2	⚐	1	1	1	**w**	1	2
⚐	2	2	2	2	2	⚑	**S**

The horses run the track counter-clockwise.

Start at "**S**" square. Ending at "w".

The horses use two (2) six-sided dice when running around the outer track.

Next, the horses use one (1) six-sided die when running around the inner.

Horses may NOT land on the same square. If a roll would put a horse on a square occupied by another horse, the arriving horse is placed just behind the occupied square on the next available empty square.

How to win: The first horse to go all the way around both the outer track, the inner track, and reach the "w" square wins. It is not necessary to reach the "w" in an exact roll.

Multiple players: Any number of players may race. Use distinct pieces for each horse. You may also tie different colored ribbon on each horse to distinguish them.

Almost Chess

Chess is a fine game—no doubt about that. Put us down as a big yes in the Gallup Pole "Is chess a cool game?" We are definitely pro chess. So, why *everything other than chess*?

The games in this book are for players who have chess sets but don't play chess. Perhaps they are not quite ready for chess or perhaps they're just looking for something a little different as a break from standard chess.

A little different this game is. "Almost Chess" is just that. It's *almost* Chess. It uses the same rules, has the same goal and plays pretty much the same except for one small detail. In this game, players use dice to move the pieces.

Object of the game: Capture the enemy king, put it into checkmate, bring the vermin dogs to their knees, make them beg for mercy—or something to that effect.

Additional equipment: Two six-sided dice.

Board setup: The board is setup the same as in standard chess.

How to play: Rather than repeat volumes of rules found in a traditional chess game, just take it as given that the moves in this game are the same except for two small differences as described next.

The first small difference is: when a player starts a turn, she will roll two six-sided dice.

The second difference is: player uses the numbers on these dice to move two playing pieces.

Two pieces are moved per turn.

The pieces are moved (if possible) the number of squares given by the dice throw.

The die can be used to move two separate pieces or added to move one piece. When combining two dice to move one character, that character may not change direction during the move.

If a legal move exists, a player must move—unless that move will put the king into check.

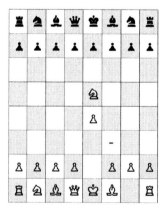

For example, if White should roll a two (2) and six (6) on her first turn, then she would be able to move resulting in the position as given in the example on the left.

You'll notice that the pawn (♟) has moved two squares forward and the knight (♞) has moved six squares following its usual dog-legged jumping fashion. The intermediate square for the knight is marked with a dash (-) in the image.

a dash (-) in the image.

Please note that knights can only be moved using a single die roll of three or a six. Or, a knight may be moved using a combination of two dice totaling either three, six, nine, or twelve—basically the roll needs to be a multiple of three.

In this example, after White's opening move, the game was left in the position as given in the image on the previous page. What if Black's first roll was a two (2) and a five (5)? This will lead to the position displayed on the right. Why did Black only move one piece? That is because there is no way to use the five (5) die in a legal move at this time. Black would need a three or six to move a knight, the longest clear path any of Black's pawns can move is four, the queen only has a path of four square in length, and each of the other pieces are blocked. Basically a die roll of five just won't work as a legal move for Black at this time.

All pieces require an exact roll to capture an opponent's piece.

Here is an important rule: At the beginning of a player's turn, prior to rolling the dice, a player may choose to substitute an automatic roll of one (1) for each or both of the dice. Thus, a player choosing to roll only one die would have a roll of whatever value chance brought for the rolled die and an automatic one on the other (non-rolled die). Or a player may choose to not roll both dice. Thus, getting an automatic roll of one (1) and one (1). As you can imagine this might be very handy when trying to capture an opponent's pieces. Remember this decision to not roll a die must be made at the beginning of one's turn. And, each die which is not rolled is automatically assumed to be a one (1).

This means that in the previous example Black could not turn that useless five (5) into a one (1). After the dice are rolled it is too late to select the automatic one option.

Let's say that after a few more moves the example board looks like the image on the left and it is now White's turn. If White were to choose an automatic (no roll required) one (1) for a die and roll the other die coming up with a random value—such as two (2)—then White could use first the one (1) to capture Black's pawn and then use the two (2) to continue moving forward—yielding the result illustrated on the right.

You can see by the (-) where White first used the one to capture Black's middle pawn, then White used the remaining die value of two to advance toward the Black King. This puts Black in jeopardy.

Fortunately Black can choose on her next turn to use one die as a one (1) and take the pawn with either the bishop, queen, or king.

An automatic (non-rolled) one (1) may only be used to capture pieces at the beginning of a player's turn before any pieces are moved. A natural one (1) may be used to capture pieces at any time during a player's turn—either before or during a move.

Consider the situation in the image above. If Black were to roll the dice and get one/one (1,1) Black could use a one (1) to advance a pawn toward White's knight, then use a second one (1) to capture that knight. This would be fine.

But, Black could not elect to manufacture two dice into ones thereby attempting the same capture of the knight. No can do. One may only capture opponent's pieces with manufactured ones (1) prior to moving.

How to win: Capture the opponent's king.

Multiple players: This game is designed for either two players or two teams.

Teams may be of any size. Two players per team is fairly typical. If you would find it fun to have 10 people on a team, then go for it. Haven't tried that yet, but it sounds fun—at least until the teams degenerate into chronic argument.

Additional example moves: In this sample to the left, if Black should roll a four/three (4,3) it would be possible for her to move the rook (♜) three squares forward, then four squares to our right capturing the White knight (♞).

Or a roll of three/two (3,2) could be used to move the bishop (♝) three squares on the diagonal capturing a White pawn (♙), then two more diagonal squares to capture a second White pawn (♙).

Or what if it were White's turn and she manufactured one die into a one (1), then rolled a natural five (5)? She could capture the Black pawn (lower right) moving her pawn out of the way of the rook, then use her rook (far right) to capture the Black rook.

"Almost Chess" is prone to sudden turns of luck and shocking ambushes from unforeseen combination moves. This gives *Almost Chess* its unique flavor.

Strategy is good, but without some luck as well, you might be in for a losing battle.

Rats and the Fox

In nature rats make good fox food. But in fairy tales, a fox might help a rat—if there is something in it for the fox.

In "Rats and the Fox," the rats strike a deal with the fox. There are two rival families of rats. Each family is trying to gain control of the central nest. If one family gains control of the nest, it can move in and keep the other rat family out—forcing them to fend for themselves in the woods.

Thus, each rat family makes a deal with a fox. If the fox helps them gain control of the central nest, then that fox will have a free lunch snacking on the rival rat family, which has been forced to live in the woods. This is what they call "mutual benefit."

Object of the game: Be the first to get four of your rats into the center nest.

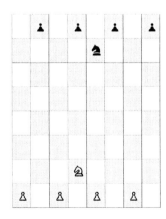

Additional equipment: Two six-sided dice.

Board setup: Each player begins with four rats in her back row and one fox placed as shown in the second row.

The center sixteen (16) squares represents the nest.

How to play: The movement of the rats and the fox is determined by two six-sided dice.

Before each roll, assign one of the die as the fox die and the other as the rat die.

During a turn, a player will move one of her rats based upon the roll of the rat die, and move her fox based upon the roll of the fox die.

The fox and rat may be moved in any order—either the fox, then a rat or a rat, then the fox.

R	R	R	R	R	R	R	R
R	F	F	F	F	F	F	R
R	F	n	n	n	n	F	R
R	F	n	n	n	n	F	R
R	F	n	n	n	n	F	R
R	F	n	n	n	n	F	R
R	F	F	F	F	F	F	R
R	R	R	R	R	R	R	R

The image on the left indicates the ring (R) for the rat's movement, the ring (F) for the fox's movement, and the nest (n) which the rats are so anxious to inhabit.

The rats and fox move in a clockwise direction only.

Only one character may occupy a square at a time.

When moving a rat or fox, it is not allowed to land on a square which is occupied—if the square indicated by the character's die roll is occupied, the character bumps ahead to the next available square—this keeps the fox and the rats moving.

For a rat to leap from the outer ring to the center nest it needs to leapfrog over the fox's back like a stepping stone.

A fox must be adjacent to a rat for that rat to use the fox's back as a stepping stone into the central nest.

In order for a rat to jump into the central nest, a player must roll a number (on the rat die) which will allow a jumping rat to land on an empty square in the nest. A rat may not land on an occupied square or get bumped ahead in the nest.

Once inside the nest, a rat will cease moving. Whatever square the rat lands on when coming into the nest is the square the rat stays in until the end of the game.

It does not matter whether a player moves her rat first or her fox first.

Let's look at an example of how the choice of which to move first might make a huge difference. Consider the game in progress on the right.

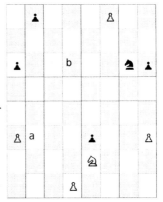

White rolls a four (4) on the fox die and a two (2) on the rat die. If White were to move a rat first, then move the fox, no rat could enter the nest. But, with this same roll White could decide to move the fox first (to square 'a') followed by a jump into the center by a rat.

Next, consider the roll (fox 5, rat 4) by Black. If Black moves the rat first, it can jump over the back of the fox (landing on square 'b') before the fox takes its turn and moves five (5) squares.

The end result of the sample rolls is shown on the left.

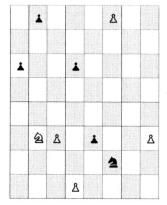

White has moved a rat into the nest by jumping across the fox's back after the fox moved into position. And Black has moved a rat into the central nest by jumping across the fox's back before it took its obligatory move.

As you may guess, this game is a combination of a little strategy and a lot of luck.

If might be wise to set a time limit on the game. For example, whoever has the most rats in the nest after thirty minutes is declared winner.

How to win: Get four of your rats into the center nest before your opponent.

Multiple players: It is possible to play this game with 2, 3, or 4 players. Many more than that and the forest (board edge) gets a bit crowded.

If you choose to play with more than two, it is wise to include pieces from a second chess set—providing differently shaped and/or differently colored pieces.

Race for Bed

Imagine a narrow passage with barely enough room for one person to move down the hall. Imagine that this hallway is a secret underground tunnel between a girl's summer camp and a boy's summer camp.

If there were such a tunnel, as you can imagine, at night when the camp counselors go to town to see a movie, kids sneak back and forth between the two camps—girls sneak over to the boys camp and boys sneak over to the girls camp.

When all sneaking is said and done, girls party at the boys camp and boys party at the girls camp. Summer life couldn't get much better. At least until the kids hear the counselors' car coming up the road. "Run, get back to your own camp, the counselors are back!"

At this point all chaos breaks loose. The boys make a mad dash home and the girls also make a mad dash home—at the exact same time. The underground tunnel becomes a busy winding passageway of kids jostling each other—all in a hurry to get back to camp before inspection—a *race for bed*.

It is hopeless to imagine all of the boys or girls will make it back to camp before inspection. The only hope the boys and girls have is for one of them to get back to the cabins and put pillows under the covers to make it look like the whole camp is safely in bed.

Object of the game: The girls are obviously trying to get one girl back to their camp so she can make up the other seven beds to look like everyone is safely in bed. And the boys are equally bent on getting a boy back to camp so that he can make up all the empty beds with pillows to look like all of the boys are safely in bed. All of this must happen before the counselors have a "We just got back from the movie and now we need to make sure the kids are okay" inspection. You may choose to play with a time limit, or you may choose to play until one of the campers (girls or boys) are all back in their beds.

Additional equipment: Two six-sided dice.

Board setup: The game begins with the board empty.

How to play: Each player has eight (8) kids caught away from camp when the counselor's return from the movie. One player has eight (8) girls caught away from bed—partying in the boy's camp. And, one player has eight (8) boys away from bed—partying in the girl's camp.

Each turn a player will roll two six-sided dice.

A player will then move two characters—one for each die rolled. Or, the two die may be combined to move a single character the sum of the two dice.

A roll of one (1) or six (6) is required to bring a boy/girl onto the board.

The girls enter the game at the corner marked with the "G".

The boys enter the game at the corner marked with the "B".

The girls exit the game at the corner marked with the "g".

The boys exit the game at the corner marked with the "b".

If during a turn a girl lands on a square occupied by a boy, the boy is sent back to begin again.

If during a turn a boy lands on a square occupied by a girl, the girl is sent back to begin again.

If two girls are on a square or two boys are on a square, that square becomes safe and it is not possible for any other characters to land on it—unless two can land at the same time.

If two boys can move so that they land on the same square at the same time, they may send two girls on that square back to camp. Or, if two girls can move so that they land on the same square at the same time they may send two boys from that square back to camp. So two pieces on the same square are safe—except from a double landing.

The image on the left shows the path taken by the boys on their journey back to the boys' camp.

This is kind of a zig-zag up the board starting on the left and finishing on the left.

The girls travel the same type of path when seen from the other player's perspective.

The image on the right shows what the girl's path looks like from the boy's point of view. If you take a board and trace it out, it will make more sense. Don't freak out. It's really not that complex.

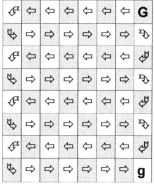

A player may exit a character from the board on any roll greater than or equal to that required to land the home square. It is not necessary to get an exact roll. Let's face it, when a girl or boy gets that close to their camp and the safety of bed before inspection, he or she is not going to dilly-dally around waiting for a special roll.

How to win: Get one (1) of your characters home to make up the beds before inspection and before the other player gets one of her characters home.

Multiple players: This game may be played with two (2) or four (4) players.

To play with four add cats and dogs—from another chess set. These camp pets (cats for girls, dogs for boys) will also have to make a mad dash back home after a visit to the other camp. In this case, any player landing on any other player's piece sends it back to the beginning.

Cops and Robber

The robber in this game has almost no chance of getting away. Sixteen cops giving chase and there is little or nowhere to run. What's a robber to do? In this, the ultimate chase-game, sixteen cops converge on a lone robber with one idea in mind: grab him and put him into cuffs.

Object of the game: The robber hopes to get away. The cops hope to capture the robber.

Additional equipment: None.

Board setup: At the beginning of the game the board is setup as indicated in the image on the left. There are sixteen cops positioned in the corners and one (white pawn) robber positioned as shown.

How to play: The robber begins the game.

When it's time for the robber to move, the player just moves the robber one square.

When it is time for the cops to move, the player must first decide which cop to move, then move that cop one square.

Characters may move up, down, left, right, and diagonal.

There is no jumping in this game.

There may be only one character on a square at a time.

On the right there are several example positions. "A" and "B" illustrate the two allowed positions for cops to capture a robber. "C" and "D" show the position just before the capturing move. In "C", the lower cop can force a capture by moving diagonally into position so that the robber is caught on the horizontal between two cops. In "D", the lower cop can force a capture by moving to the right so that the robber is caught between two cops on the vertical.

On the left are three examples of how the robber may take out cops. In "A", the robber may move diagonally between two horizontal cops forcing them from the game. In "B", the robber may remove two cops by stepping to the left between the two vertical cops. In "C", the robber may remove two cops by stepping between two cops on the diagonal.

You will notice that the cops may only capture a robber on the horizontal and the vertical. But, the robber can take cops from the game on the horizontal, the vertical, and the diagonal. This gives the robber a bit of an edge that might even compensate for the fact that he is outnumbered sixteen to one at the beginning of the game.

How to win: The cops win by capturing the robber.

The robber will win by either evading the cops until they get disgusted and give up, or by removing enough of the cops that it becomes impossible to capture the robber.

Multiple players: For three or more players, add an additional robber to the game for each additional player.

In games of three or more, cops are not removed from the game when a robber steps between two cops. In this case, the two cops are returned to any two empty starting squares. Now the aim of the game becomes "be the last robber free." Any number of players may cooperate to play the cops.

Claude Needham

Treasure Hunt

Pirates, gold miners, kids on an Easter Egg hunt, everyone loves finding treasure. That's the theme to this simple game.

Object of the game: The object of *Treasure Hunt* is to find your opponent's three treasures before they find your three buried treasures.

Additional equipment: Small stickers or dots.

Board setup: The setup of pieces is the same as in standard chess.

How to play: To begin the game, both player will avert their eyes (look away) while the other hides three treasures. A treasure is marked by a small sticker or dot stuck to the bottom of a chess piece.

Each turn, a player will guess under which of her opponent's pieces there is a buried treasure.

It is not okay to touch the other player's pieces. After making a guess, your opponent will pick up the guessed-at piece and check the bottom.

If a player guesses correctly, the piece is removed from the board and placed in the guessing player's hoard.

If the piece does not have a treasure underneath, it is returned to the board.

How to win: Guess the location and get three treasures first.

Multiple players: In games of three or more, one player is elected to control all 32 pieces. This player hides nine stickers (or dots) under nine pieces for nine buried treasures.

The remaining players all try to be first to win three treasures (stickers/dots.)

Special options: At parties, the stickers (or dots) could represent real treasures such as candies, sweets, or perhaps kisses. Depends on the party, I suppose.

Scavenger Hunt

Whether it is raining or not, it is always fun to go on a scavenger hunt.

Object of the game: Be the first to collect all of your pieces.

Additional equipment: One six-sided die.

Board setup: At the beginning of the game, players take turns placing the "back row" (rooks, knights, bishops, king, & queen) around the outside edge of the board—except for the four corners. The four corners are off limits. Then, each player will place one pawn somewhere in the inner circle of the board.

How to play: Players move only within the first inner circle of the game board—marked with arrows in the image.

Each turn, a player rolls one six-sided die and moves her pawn that number of squares around the inner circle.

If the White pawn lands next to one of the White scavenger pieces, then White collects it.

If the Black pawn lands next to one of the Black scavenger pieces, then Black collects it.

If a player lands upon an opponent's piece, that opponent returns one collected piece to the board's outer edge and then places her "bumped" pawn on any square in the inner circle.

If (as in a corner) two pieces are adjacent to the pawn, then a player may collect both pieces.

By the way, it is probably a very bad idea to place a scavenger piece in any of the four corners. This would be a bad idea, because it is not possible to collect the piece from the corners.

How to win: Collect all of your scavenger pieces before your opponent does. Because of the extreme reversals of fortune which can occur during this game, it might be a good idea to set a timer and have whoever has the most scavenger pieces at the moment the timer goes off declared the winner.

Multiple players: Two, three, or four may easily play. Just add in pieces from other chess sets as required.

Attack of the Mambo Line

In this snail-paced game, two Mambo lines face-off in a dancing showdown—attacking each other with dedicated vigor.

Object of the game: Reduce the other Mambo line to a single dancer.

Additional equipment: None.

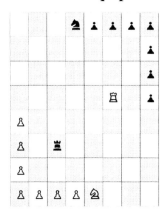

Board setup: The image on the left illustrates the initial game setup. The two Mambo lines start in opposite corners as shown. The two rooks in the center are placed randomly (or strategically) by the players one at a time before the game play begins. Thus, each game will not necessarily look like the one to the left; it depends on how players choose to place their rooks.

How to play: Every turn the Mambo line moves one square forward—up, down, left, or right—not diagonal.

Mambo lines may not pass through the immovable blocks (rooks 🨣).

The Mambo lines move in a "follow-the-leader" fashion—segment after segment, keeping to the existing squares.

If a player may not move her Mambo line forward, she will

lose one segment from the end of the line. One segment is lost for each turn the line is blocked from moving forward.

If the head of one Mambo line is able to move onto the tail of the other Mambo line, that dancer is eliminated from the line.

How to win: If a player reduces the other Mambo line to a single dancer, the game is over and the longer Mambo line wins. Or, after a set time period, the longest Mambo line wins.

Multiple players: Give it a try. We'd suggest using five (5) or six (6) dancers in a Mambo line when playing with more than two players.

Play hint: A quick way to move your Mambo line is to move the front Mambo dancer into whatever square is decided upon, then remove the Mambo dancer from the end of the line and place it in the square vacated by the lead Mambo dancer. This will eliminate the need to mess around with scooting every dancer one square.

If you prefer scooting each dancer forward, please feel free. It's kinda' fun moving them around.

Moving Day

Isn't life grand when things have a way of working out just so darn perfect.

On Monday, two families put an ad in the paper looking to sublet their apartments so they can move to the other side of town.

On Tuesday, these two families call each other by coincidence, and wouldn't you know it, they each live on opposite sides of town in the exact neighborhoods each is hoping to move into.

On Wednesday, both families sign leases and agree to move — starting tomorrow.

On Thursday, they start the move, Family A leaving their home, moving to Home B; Family B leaving their home, moving to Home A.

With things going so well, the fathers of each family decide a little bet is in order. They each bet that their family is the best movers and that they can move into a new home the fastest.

The bet is: whoever loses has to pay for all of the moving expenses.

Whether you care about saving the moving expenses or just want the bragging rights—the race is on.

Object of the game: Get your family moved into your new home before the other family moves into theirs.

Additional equipment: None.

Board setup: The image on the left illustrates the beginning setup for the game. Family A at home packing boxes. Family B at home packing boxes. Both packed and ready to run for their new homes.

How to play: During a turn, a player moves one family member one square up, down, left, right, or diagonal.

Family members may jump any other family member—from either home.

The example on the right illustrates a very long sequence of jumps. Black may jump all the way from the upper right to the lower left. First to 1, then 2, then 3, then 4, then finally to 5.

How to win: Get all of your family members into the new apartment.

Multiple players: This game works with either 2 or 4 players. When playing with 4, add pieces from another chess set—one with different shapes. Set them up in opposite corners and let the jumping begin.

Four in a Row

This game has been played from ancient times into the present. Heck, as far as I know, cavemen might have played this game with stones on a cave floor. Well, maybe not. But who can prove otherwise?

As a culture, we have some silly notion that anyone born before the electron age is either moronic, an idiot, or both. It is definitely unusual for anyone to give peoples from ancient times credit for inventing a game—even one that uses nothing more complicated than pebbles and a floor.

Think about it: pebbles weren't discovered just last week, and we've had floors for at least a month or two—maybe even longer.

So it's possible that those hairy dudes and dudettes could have invented something as technologically simple as *Four in a Row*.

In any case, I wouldn't want to get caught cheating one of those guys. They carried big sticks and weren't afraid to smack each other with them; at least, if you are to believe all those old-time movies from the 1950s.

Object of the game: Get four pieces in a row either horizontal, vertical, or along a diagonal.

Additional equipment: There is no additional equipment required for this game.

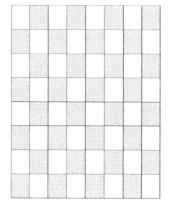

Board setup: In *Four in a Row* we begin with an empty playing board with no pieces on it—not unlike a fresh-swept cave floor.

How to play: Decide who is to go first. This can either be through mutual agreement or the roll of dice.

Players, one at a time, place pieces on the playing board.

A "four in a row" may be vertical, horizontal, or diagonal.

The image on the right illustrates a possible game part way through a match.

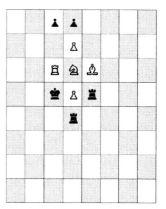

In this example, Black is doomed to lose. White has an open-ended three. No matter which end Black blocks, White will get four in a row.

If all 32 pieces are played without one or the other player winning, that game is declared a draw and a new game is started.

How to win: Get four pieces in a row.

Multiple players: This is not really a multi-player type of game. Maybe that's why the cave people didn't play it? Maybe they preferred group games that the whole family could join.

Medic

The game of chess was developed to teach men about waging wars and strategies for winning. One military occupation overlooked during the creation of chess was the medic. Anyone who watches re-runs of old television shows will be familiar with the show M.A.S.H. and just how important the medic is. It is the medic that patches up men so they can go back out onto the front lines to be knocked down again.

Object of the game: Keep your men standing.

Additional equipment: One six-sided die, one eight-sided die, and counters such as stones.

Board setup: Each player has a front line with eight soldiers and one medic running around in the back field patching up any soldiers that fall during battle.

How to play: The game play is divided into three game cycles that repeat over and over until one or the other player wins.

The first cycle is composed of killing, the second cycle is dedicated to healing, and the third game cycle is reserved for scoring.

In game cycle "1", an eight-sided die is used to determine which, if any, of the opponent's soldiers are hit.

There are eight columns, eight soldiers, and on an eight-sided die there are eight numbers. Pretty straight-forward. The only trick is remembering to count from the left. If a player rolls a three then the opponent's third soldier from the left is "hit."

When a soldier is hit, it is knocked-down, i.e. laid down on the board as a casualty. By the way, if a soldier is already down, then the die roll is more or less wasted since the soldier is already as down as it can get.

During game cycle "2", each player rolls a six-sided die to move their respective medics back and forth. The medic may move left or right and "bounce" off the edge of the board to finish up the die count.

If the medic manages to land on a square behind a downed soldier, the medic can revive that downed soldier, standing them up to fight another day.

Finally, in game cycle "3", score is calculated for that round. To determine the score, the number of standing soldiers for each player is compared. The player with the greater number of standing soldiers receives a stone (or counter) for each soldier they have in excess of their opponent. For example, if Player "A" has 6 standing soldiers and Player "B" has 4 standing soldiers, then Player "A" is awarded 2 stone counters.

In summary, first we have a lot of shooting and knocking-down of soldiers. This is followed by medics scurrying about healing as best as possible. Finally, the score of standing soldiers are compared.

Player "A" tries to knock down a soldier of Player "B," and Player "B" tries to knock down a soldier of Player "A." Then Player "A" tries to heal one of her downed soldiers, and Player "B" tries to heal one of her downed soldiers.

Following this double exchange the score is calculated.

On the right is an illustration demonstrating the numbers which a player must roll to knock down a soldier on the opposite side. You'll notice that the numbers run in opposite directions. This is because that which is left to one player is not the same as that which is left to the other player. Sit down with an actual game board and you'll figure it out.

1	2	3	4	5	6	7	8
8	7	6	5	4	3	2	1

In the example to the left, if White rolled a 5 (on the six-sided die) she would be able to heal her soldier on the left (by bouncing off the edge). The "?" represents downed soldiers.

How to win: A player may win by being the first to collect twenty stones or knock down all of the opponent's soldiers.

Multiple players: Two is best.

Claude Needham

Corporate Ladder

As rumor has it, the way to climb the corporate ladder is over the backs of others. That's how this game is played. You can climb over friends who cooperate, or you can climb over competitors that object. In either case, the goal is to get to the top and it doesn't matter who you have to climb over to get there.

Object of the game: Get one of your executives to the top of the corporate ladder.

Additional equipment: One six-sided die.

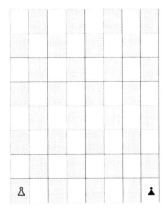

Board setup: The board begins as illustrated on the left. There is one White pawn on the left, and a Black pawn on the right. In addition, each player has seven extra executives (pawns) waiting in the wings.

How to play: Each turn, a player rolls one six-sided die.

The player may move any of her executives that happen to be on the board either left or right.

If an executive lands on the back of another, that executive moves up the corporate ladder one row. The executive that was landed upon does not get sent home, nor is it moved up the ladder. It just stands there looking bewildered.

Black and White work their way up the corporate ladder starting from the same bottom row. Because of this, it might be friendlier to sit on the same side of the table.

On most rows of the corporate ladder, when an executive moves up to the next row, it will leave one fewer on the row it is leaving. However, the bottom row is special. Each time an executive moves up the corporate ladder from the bottom row, another executive is moved in from the wings (until all eight executives are in play). If a White executive moves up from the bottom row, then another White executive is moved in from the wings. If a Black executive moves up from the bottom row, then a Black executive is moved in from the wings. If, however, a player has already moved all eight of her executives into the game, then an executive from the other player's team is moved into the game. While executives are left in the wings, there will never be more than, nor less than, two executives in the bottom row.

The image to the right illustrates one possible game.

Let's suppose it is Black's next move and Black rolls a two. Black may move the executive in the second row two squares to the right and jump to the third row over the back of the white pawn. Or, if Black rolls a three, Black may move the executive in the first row three squares to the left and jump

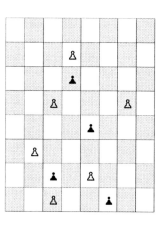

to the second row. But, since the second row square is occupied, the executive will jump over that executive's back as well, moving to the third tier of the corporation.

How to win: Get an executive to the top row of the corporate ladder.

Multiple players: 2, 3, or 4 players can play. After that it gets a little confusing. If more than two players are in the game, establish by agreement before the game begins which squares the additional executives will use for starting.

Claude Needham

Ghosts

What if ghosts could help other ghosts to "move on" into the light. Maybe ghosts can help each other ascend out of the limbo of earthly attachments. In fact, maybe there are whole teams of ghosts that make this their life's eh... after-life's work. This ghostly Traveler's Aid Society could run about assisting other ghosts past the spooky realm into the "somewhere else realm."

Object of the game: Assist more of your opponent's ghosts into the next realm than they do yours.

Additional equipment: None.

Board setup: The image on the left illustrates the beginning setup.

How to play: Players decide who goes first. This can be through mutual agreement, or drawing lots. or rolling dice, or loser goes first, or hot potato, or arm wrestling. It really doesn't matter. Just figure it out.

Each player moves one ghost one square each turn.

A ghost may move up, down, left, or right—not diagonally.

If a ghost is surrounded by two ghosts—either horizontally or vertically—the surrounded ghost is sent into the next realm.

Move Examples: If the ghost in the upper left were to move onto square "a", the White ghost would be removed from the board and sent on its way to the next realm.

Referring to the image on the right, if the White ghost were to move onto square "b", nothing would happen. The ghosts were already there so there is no capture.

If the White ghost in the lower left were to move onto the square "c", nothing would happen because it is diagonal, and the ghosts have to be surrounded either horizontally or vertically.

If the White ghost in the lower right were to move onto square "d", then the Black ghost would be sent on to the next realm and removed from the board.

How to win: Send more of your opponent's ghosts to the next realm.

Multiple players: This is basically a two player game. A new version coming out in the second edition of this book will be suitable for more than two players.

Relay Races

Relay races are great fun. They are a wonderful team effort in which individual achievement can be appreciated, while keeping the group goal as the primary focus.

Object of the game: Get your runners back and forth and home before your opponent's runners beat you.

Additional equipment: Two six-sided dice.

Board setup: The illustration on the left shows a typical relay race beginning setup.

On the board for each team is one pawn ready and set to go. Behind the line at the top and bottom are the other runners waiting to take their turn in the relay race.

How to play: Player each roll a six-sided die—at the same time. This will give a better feel of fast competition.

Players then move their respective runner the number of squares indicated on their die.

If the die roll is in excess of the number of squares required to make it to the end of the column, then the next runner uses the remaining numbers.

If in the image on the right White were to roll a five, the first pawn would use up two of the five to get past the last square. The next runner (also a pawn in this example) would then use the remainder to run three squares.

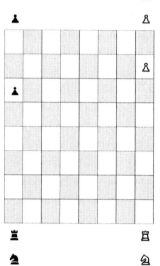

This game is mostly a game of rolling high numbers combined with the rudimentary ability to remember which direction you should be running.

How to win: Get all of your runners through the relay.

Multiple players: Up to eight players may participate. Other chess sets will be required to make up the required pieces.

Lion and the Goats

Lions are big, fast, and have monstrous jaws, but, goats are not entirely defenseless—they have cooperation and stubborn persistence on their side. In this game it is a toss up whether the goats will all get eaten, or perhaps, they may push the lion into a corner rendering it incapable of munching and lunching on other goats.

Object of the game: The goats try to surround the lion making it impossible to be eaten (goats are not fond of being eaten). The lion tries to jump goats and eat them (lions are fond of eating goats).

Additional equipment: None.

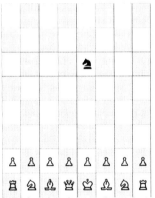

Board setup: The image on the left shows the standard beginning setup. A bunch of goats and one lion.

How to play: The lion starts the game by advancing toward the goats.

The lion may move up, down, left, right and diagonal.

The goats may move up, left, and right—not down nor diagonal.

Lions may eat a goat by jumping it either on the horizontal, vertical, or diagonal.

A lion may jump (eat) a goat if the lion is adjacent to the goat and there is an empty square on the other side of the goat.

A lion may jump any number of goats in sequence as long as there is an empty square inbetween for each jump.

A lion may not jump a goat that does not have an empty square on the other side.

Goats do not jump.

How to win: If the lion eats all of the goats or eats enough goats that it becomes impossible for the goats to win, then the lion wins. If the goats crowd around the lion and make it impossible for it to move or jump any goats, then the goats win.

Multiple players: For three players: split the goats into two herds assigning one herd to player "a" and one herd to player "b". The third player would be the lion.

For four players: Add eight goats to the herd for a total of twenty-four goats. Split the herd in two so that two players each have twelve goats. Add an extra lion so that two players have one lion each.

Cleaning Day

Back by popular demand we have competitive cleaning. Word on the street has it that Xtreme cleaning is being considered by the Olympic committee for inclusion in the next Olympic games. The hot debate is whether it should be in the winter games or summer games.

At the moment there is no consensus about in which season the sport belongs. All we know for sure is that we can't wait for competitive cleaning to take its place right alongside Olympic dominoes and Xtreme sleeping.

Object of the game: Be the first to pick up all your trash.

Additional equipment: None.

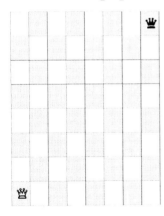

Board setup: At the beginning of the game the queens are placed in opposite corners. You may use the two kings if you can manage to get them to clean.

How to play: During the first phase of the game, players take turns placing bits of trash for their opponents to deal with.

White will place the eight Black pawns for the Black queen to pick up and Black will place the eight White pawns for the White queen to pick up.

The image to the right illustrates a sample of how a board might look after White and Black finish placing the 16 bits of trash around the board for each other to pick up.

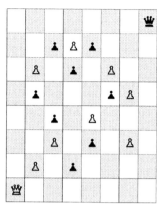

After the trash is placed, the two queens attempt to pick up their respective trash the fastest.

White queen will pick up the White trash (pawns).

Black queen will pick up the Black trash (pawns).

A queen may move left, right, up or down—not diagonally.

A queen may move any number of squares unless blocked by a piece of trash.

If a queen runs into a piece of trash of her own color, that trash is picked up.

If a queen runs into a piece of trash of the opposite color, she is blocked and cannot proceed further in that direction.

Queens get one move per turn. A move may be any number of uninterrupted squares in an up, down, left or right direction.

Queens may not leap, or otherwise go through each other.

How to win: The first to collect all eight pieces of trash wins.

Multiple players: Add pieces from other chess sets.

d20 Chess

In *d20 Chess* the pieces are setup as in standard chess. The moves are the same as in standard chess; the game would almost be standard chess except for a few simple little rule changes. As you play *d20 Chess,* you'll soon discover these so-called minor rule changes make a big difference in how the game unfolds.

If you've played any RPG (role playing games), then the name *d20 Chess* should be just about enough to explain the game. For the rest of you, the rules below will hopefully give enough detail to get started.

Object of the game: Capture the enemy king, put it into checkmate, bring the vermin dogs to their knees, make them plead for mercy—or something to that effect.

Additional equipment: One d20 (twenty-sided die).

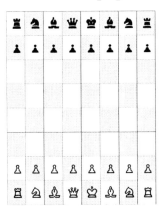

Board setup: The board is setup the same as in standard chess.

How to play: Rather than repeat volumes of rules found in a traditional chess game, just take it as given that the moves in this game are the same.

Players move the same number of spaces as in normal chess; players move the same directions.

Here's the big difference: when a player decides to "take" an opponent's piece instead of automatically "taking" the piece, both players roll a d20 to determine who wins.

If the attacking player wins, the opponent's piece is removed from the board and the attacker takes up residence in the captured square—as in normal chess.

If the attacking player loses, then the attacking piece retreats to whatever square it started from just before the attack.

When rolling to determine winner of a match between pieces, the highest number wins—and the tie goes to the defender.

The following adjustments are made to a roll depending upon the pieces involved and attack mode.

Queen – add 7 when attacking, add 5 when defending.

Bishop– add 6 when attacking, add 6 when defending.

Knight– add 5 when attacking, add 3 when defending.

Rook – add 3 when attacking, add 10 when defending.

Pawn – add 0 when attacking, add 0 when defending.

King – subtract 3 when attacking, add 8 when defending.

Optional rules: If you are up to the record keeping challenge, you may wish to add a bonus to pieces as they win matches. For example, each time a pawn wins in a match, add +2 to its attacking and defending rolls. We leave this as an exercise for the more adventuresome of our readers. By the way, please don't hesitate to contact us with any interesting optional rules you happen to develop.

Afterword

By now you have tried many, most, all, or at least some of the games suggested within the pages of this book.

As you work your way through the book trying different games, you will notice that the skill level and demand varies from game to game. Some are simple chase games requiring little more than the ability to roll a die and count to six. Other games call upon strategy and forethought rivaling that of chess. This is meant to be a family book with a little something for everyone—a spectrum of games for every age group and gaming skill level.

The goal of the book was to provide games other than chess which may be played using a standard chess set and board.

In case you are wondering where the inspiration for this book came from, it was selling *Dog & Cat* chess sets at a street fair.

So many young children—girls especially—fell in love with the "cute chess set" only to have their hopes of taking one home dashed by the common parental refrain, "But dear, you don't play chess; it will just go to waste."

Well, that problem has been solved. Now, girls and boys everywhere may visit their local chess supply store, throw the door open and declare in a voice plain and loud for anyone to hear: "I'd like a Dog & Cat chess set please, for I intend to play games. In fact, I believe I'll have a Civil War chess set as well. And, don't worry about slipping in any of those there chess books, for I will be playing everything other than chess.

Claude Needham

You see my good man, I am chess-challenged and darn proud of it."

As you may guess, many players who begin playing the non-chess games from *Everything Other Than Chess* move on to learn and appreciate chess itself—as it should be.

We like to think of *Everything Other Than Chess* as a way to justify purchase of a "way too cute to pass up" chess set, and as a stepping stone toward playing chess.

Glossary

Die: The singular form of "dice." Example: "He selected one die, put it in his hand, selected another die, put that into his hand along with the first die, gave them a blow for good luck, and rolled the dice."

Black: Black (and White) are names for the two opposite sides of the chess pieces. If you happen to own a Civil War themed chess set then the pieces will actually be blue and gray. So Black and White do not necessarily refer to the actual colors of the chess pieces. Rather, these are convenient nicknames for the two sides of the chess set.

Row 1: The rows are numbered relative to the player starting with the row closest to the player. This means that row 1 for Black will be the row closest to the player who is using the Black pieces and row 8 will be the row furthest from Black. Because White is sitting on the opposite side of the board, the row 1 for Black happens to be the row which White would call 8 and Black's row 8 would happen to be the row which White considers to be row 1. Don't worry, once you begin playing it's not that confusing.

Column 1: Throughout this book, whenever reference is made to a column number, the convention is to begin numbering with one (1) on the far left from the perspective of the player in question. Thus, what is column one for White is column eight for Black and

Claude Needham

vice versa.

Outer Ring: The outer ring of the board is made up of those rows and columns closest to the edge of the board. In the image on the right we have marked the squares in the outer ring with small "o"s.

o	o	o	o	o	o	o	o
o	i	i	i	i	i	i	o
o	i					i	o
o	i					i	o
o	i					i	o
o	i					i	o
o	i	i	i	i	i	i	o
o	o	o	o	o	o	o	o

Inner Ring: The inner ring of the board is made up of those squares just inside of the outer ring. In the image to the right we have marked the squares in this inner ring with an "i".

Center of Board: The center of the board, depending upon the game in question, will either be the middle four squares or the middle sixteen squares.

About the Author

Born: 9-2-51, Sacramento, CA.
Educated: A lot.
PhD.: Molecular Biophysics.

Vocations/Avocations: artist, writer, scientist, editor, gold miner, teacher, sculptor, painter, dancer, tree planter, programmer, web developer, jeweler, screen writer, freelance press, game designer, museum curator, and....
Let it suffice to say that I came from a very creative family environment which valued the sciences and the arts—both being equally respected as natural by-products of a creative, questing mind. I seem to recall lots of skate-boarding, bike riding, wooden sticks whittled into guns, fishing, camping, toy rockets, chemistry and Erector sets, broken glass mosaics, poker, tunnel forts, crystal radios, dirt clod fights, Risk, toy figures, model airplanes, Stratego, reading, reading, reading, and the ever present *Mad* magazine. You know... the usual.

Currently my time is spent in a kaleidoscopic scurry between writing, sculpting, programming, painting, web-design, consulting, game design, jewelry, gaming, freelance press, and miscellaneous art projects.

If the past is anything to go by, which I believe it is, then my future is pretty indeterminate—at least insofar as specifics are concerned. Most likely I will be eternally involved in one creative project after another. What the nature of each project may be, or what the specific manifestation of this creativity

Claude Needham

will be, remains to be seen.

If you are wondering about other publications, below you'll find a list of books in public editions (yes, this implies books in private editions not readily available.)

Partial list of books:

Handbook for the Recently Deceased

Just Because Club

Any Game Cookbook—Recipes for Spiritual Gaming

Partial list of games:

AnyGame^tm—A little of all games.

Zenn—3d fly-through game of Zen.

Alphabet—3d player point of view alphabet trainer.

Quzzles—Quizical little puzzles (Win98)

Touch a Rock—A Zen romp through repetition

Pre-Cog—Esp trainer (Win98)

gMaze—Choice Point Adventures Engine and games

Apperception—Esp and Memory trainer (Win98)

ArtDom—Fun little abstract art program. (Win98)

No22—Drumming with a difference (Win98)

Monotony—Board game.

Dear *Everything Other Than Chess* Reader:

If you have any questions or comments for the author or the publisher of this book, you are welcome to contact Gateways. We will do our best to answer your questions about these games and supply any equipment mentioned as necessary in this book.

Gateways Books & Tapes
P.O. Box 370-EC
Nevada City, CA 95959
Phone: (530) 271-2239
Fax: (530) 272-0184

Email: info@gatewaysbooksandtapes.com

Websites:

www.gatewaysbooksandtapes.com

www.gamexx.com

www.spiritualgaming.com

Claude Needham

Chess Player II by E.J. Gold
22" x 15" Rives BFK
Serigraph signed and numbered, edition of 75
Chess Player II © 1987 - 2006, Heidelberg Editions International
All Rights Reserved
Available from www.hei-art.com

Page 84

Final Thanks

I first met E.J. Gold through our mutual involvement in physics and my growing interest in macro-gaming.

I have since come to know him as artist, writer, sculptor, teacher, and chess master.

In case you are wondering, not that I expect you to be, it was *Dog & Cat* chess sets from his shop that I was selling in the aforementioned street fair, which lead to the development of this book. So, if you enjoy any of the games in this book, feel free to drop by his website—TheChessMaster.com—and say hello.

By the way, you can also reach me through the same contact form. If you're having any trouble with deciphering a particular game's instructions—don't bang your head against the wall—drop a line through TheChessMaster.com and I'll try to help out.

Claude Needham